ISBN 978-1-60920-124-5
Printed in the United States
©2021 Dianne Martin
All Rights Reserved

Library of Congress-In-Publication Data

API
Ajoyin Publishing Inc.
P.O. Box 342
Three Rivers, MI 49093

Please direct your inquires to Ajoyin2014@gmail.com

AJOYIN
PUBLISHING inc.
Where joy finds a voice
1.888.273.4JOY
http://www.ajoyin.com

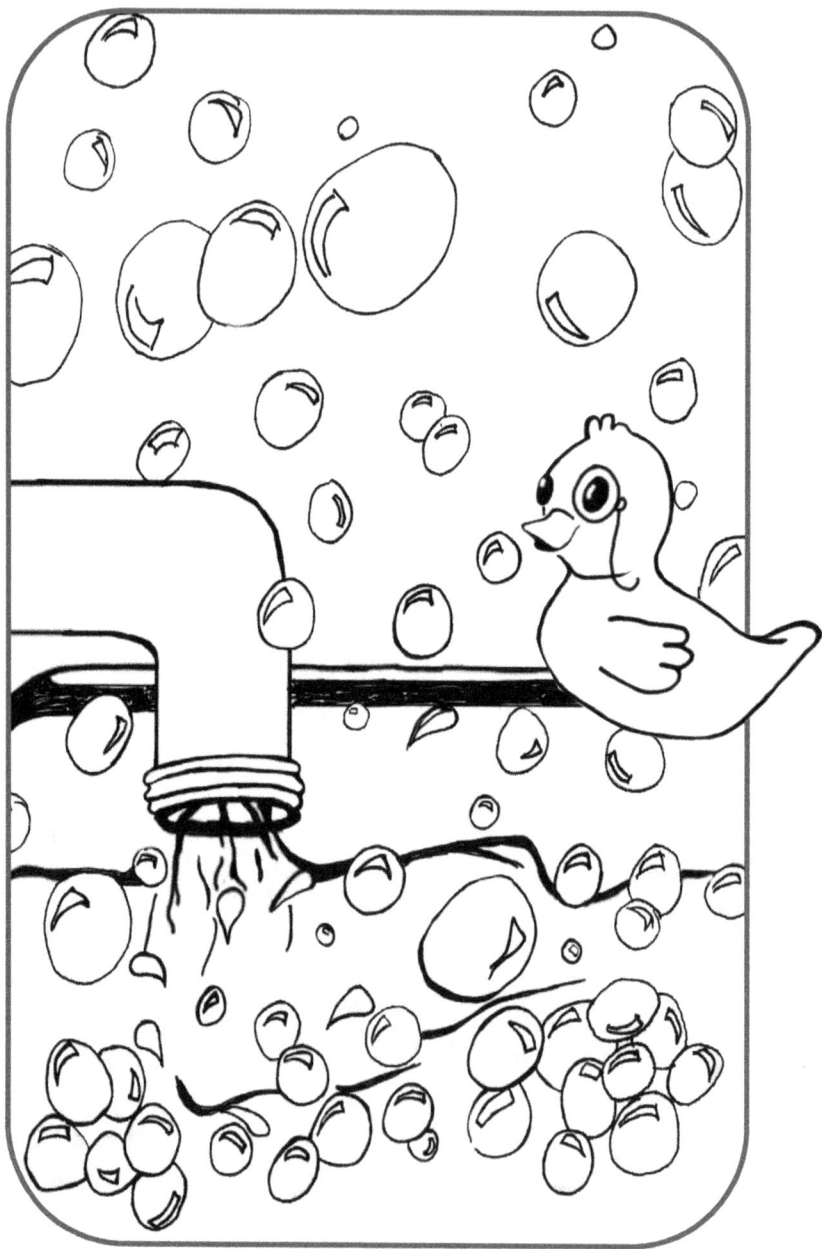

The Adventure Begins...
With the Twins

They had done it again!

The twins, Adam and Luke,
had flooded the bathroom floor with
too much soap and too much water.

I should know— I'm an eyewitness;
My name is DC Duck.
As a duck, I know a lot about water.
I was made for water.

I live in the water, at least during bath time.
Then sometimes Adam or Luke decide
to take me to bed with them for the night.
But I belong in the bathroom, near the
water, and eventually I find my way
back there.

This time the twins had really done
it though! They'd invited their friend
Ethan to come over to play.

They forgot Ethan hates water. He <u>really</u>
doesn't like it.

Let me start at the beginning.

Adam and Luke are identical six year old twin brothers. Their parents often have trouble knowing who is Adam and who is Luke.

Adam is the oldest brother by four minutes, although I've heard their mother say it seemed a lot longer than four minutes to her. But the doctor told her it was only four minutes and doctors are always right.

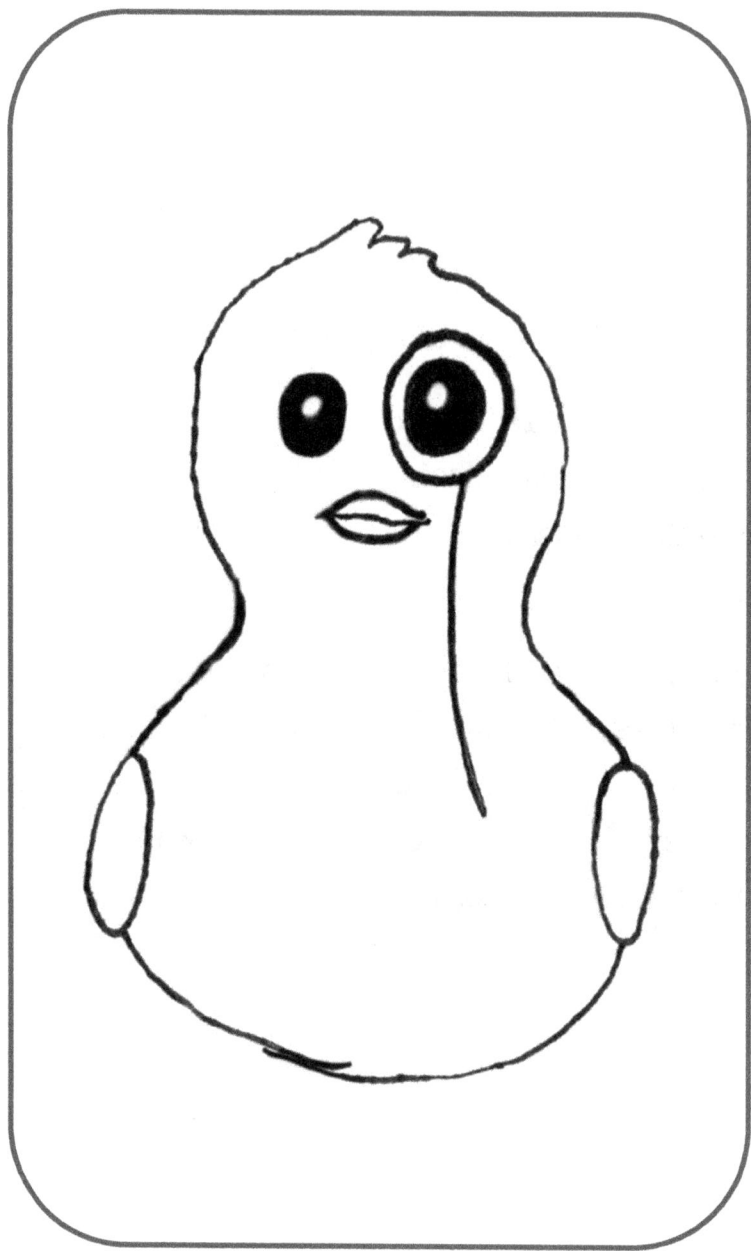

I was a gift to Adam and Luke when
they were born from someone who didn't
believe the boy's mom was really going
to have twins. They bought one duck,
that's me, DC Duck, short for
Detective Carlton.

The twins have loved baths since they
first came home from the hospital.
Some say it's not normal to "take to water
like a duck" from birth. I personally don't
understand why not, but then, I AM a duck.

Adam and Luke had visitors often and lots
of them. Some of them were older
and some were the same age as the twins
like Ethan.

I was aware very early in the three friend's
relationship that Ethan did not like water.
Whenever water spilled at the dinner table,
Ethan would scream, then run and hide.
On summer days the twins would splash in
a small pool of water while Ethan stayed
in the house and read books.

One very hot afternoon, in the middle
of the day, the three friends were quietly
looking at books when Adam leaned over
to Luke and whispered, "Let's take baths!"

"Great idea," said Luke, "but what about
Ethan? You know how much he hates water."

"We'll trick him," said Adam.
"Just follow me."

I watched as Adam distracted Ethan by talking to him about a book they had read.

Luke quietly slipped into the bathroom for the promised prank they were going to play on Ethan.

Luke turned on the faucet to the bathtub full blast. He'd poured half a bottle of bubble bath into the running water when he realized he was pouring in Mom's special bubbly soap and not the one they usually used.

To hide the evidence of his big mistake, he poured in ALL Moms' special bubble bath and threw the bottle away. He then rummaged through the bathroom closet for bath toys.

I could see this was going to be a big mess.
Lucky for me, I'd been left on the window
sill of the room after their bath last night
and Luke didn't see me. But I saw
everything. I was a witness to their crime.

I was right. It was a mess, a BIG mess!

Luke yelled, "Ready"!

Adam took off for the bathroom forgetting
all about Ethan.

I watched as Ethan, now aware
of the twins' plan, slowly sneak
closer to an open window.
I watched as he quietly snuck
out and ran home as fast as his
feet could carry him.

I witnessed the whole mess. I watched their mom when she entered the bathroom and looked at the BIG mess.

She was mad!

I can't tell you how this ended for Adam and Luke. I will only say they now take baths without bubbles. Ethan still comes over to play, but he won't go near the bathroom unless he has to, and he makes sure the twins are where he can see them when he does.

As for me, I saw the whole thing happen
from the window of the bathroom and
I doubt it will happen again, at least not
unless it's another hot afternoon and Adam
and Luke decide to take a bath in the middle
of another day.

From the Author:

My first published book, A Fishy Story, was written
to my nine grandchildren. DC Duck and the
Adventure Twins is dedicated to my now fifteen year
old twin grandsons. The incident recorded in this story
never actually happened, at least not to my knowledge,
but it could have.

Love you lots Adam and Luke,

Grandma Martin

About the Illustrator:

My niece, Anneka, is the illustrator for this story.
She is fifteen years old and a home schooled sophomore
with interests in art, music, and theatre.

Thank you Anneka for working with me
on this project.

Aunt Dianne

www.ingramcontent.com/pod-product-compliance
Lightning Source LLC
Chambersburg PA
CBHW071808020426
42331CB00008B/2435